Tales of Light and Dust

Lindsay Pettifor

To Dee,

With all my love & thanks,

Lindsay xx

Copyright © 2023 by Lindsay Pettifor

ISBN: 9798393847630

Published by www.publishandprint.co.uk

All rights reserved. No part of this book may be used or reproduced in any manner whatsoever without written permission from the author.

Front cover and author photograph by Simon Pettifor

Contents

One Day Hill	1
Communing With Trees	4
Cwm Felin	6
Bluebells	9
Cloud Burst	10
Aber Mawr	12
Stump	14
Lyme Bay	16
Transience Blues	20
Beach Light	22
Harvest Moon, Torcross	23
Kings Thorn	24
Sun Down	26
Moonshine	27
The Pool	28
Wasteland	29
Bird Spirit Land	30
Trapeze	32
Nectar	34
Pearl	36
Starman	38

Triptych	39
Guardian Angel	40
Afternoon, with Butterflies	42
Forget-me-not	44
On Malvern	46
Freesias	50
White Dwarf	51
Memento Mori	52
Ash	57

One Day Hill

Today we climbed One Day Hill.

A sharp, azure sky,
Frost laced on the skeletoned leaves of dead ferns
that crumple and scrunch under our step,
shying away from the warming rays of the gathering sun.
The tips of the pine trees whisper at our approach,
Bending their heads,
Snowdrops at their feet,
and sough at our passing.

The lake is still –
filigrees and stars of ice trace its reaches,
Broken only by the murmuring promise of the return of spring
brought in on the ceaseless trickling of the peat-black stream
that meanders and feeds the damp copse,
verdant and moss-green and bright.

Fragile shoots of bluebells and daffodils nestle in tree roots,
Their sap-green and tender stems belie the strength of self-
   belief that they will overcome the treacheries of winter.

The sun is bright and full of promise,
highlighting pockets of lichen-dusted bark on the hazels and
   oaks,
kaleidoscopic flashes of light and colour on the underskirts of
   the wood.
The track beneath our feet climbs along the crumbling

    sandstone ridge and our footsteps are cushioned on the
       dust of ancient rock
and the soft mulch of winter leaves.

A sudden break in the treeline
stretches out the view from our vantage point
across hazily patch-worked fields and wooded hills
as far as the eye can see.

And then I know this place.

I recognise the folds of land
that make up the field that lies before us,
I follow the pattern of hedgerows
that map out a tracery of contour lines, framing my reference.
I remember the house that blends and nestles
into the hill at our side.

Every day I saw these,
In the changing shadows of early dawn and evening light:

The last eyeful-lungful gasp and flash of bright green space
   before the passage of -

- speeding train racing through concrete and tarmac, brick
and steel, dead ends and rubbish and graffiti tattoos, soot-
stained, water-stained, crumbling, rusting, abandoned
factories, junkyards and rows of tiny fake boxes all with
satellite dishes and blank glassy thousand-yard stares
crammed shoulder to shoulder under a diminishing louring
metallic-grey sky, closing in and suffocating, pressing on the

throat, the eye, the heart until it feels like you're going under for the last time -

And then

The releasing, expanding inhalation of my return,
The shocking liberty of wide horizon as the trainline
blooms into countryside and space,
into sky and green and breath once more,
Fulfilling the oath of peace and home.

Each day my eye would never tire of seeking out
this hill, this house, this view.
Touchstone and amulet and prayer,
A talisman on my journey out,
A validation on my journey home.
And every day I renewed my pledge,
My promise to myself:
'One day, I will climb that hill'.

Today, we climbed One Day Hill.

Communing With Trees

Damask pink candles in spring,
Draping, arched branches,
Graceful as water.
Offering cool comfort, a safe cocoon.
Is this why?

Crisp, splayed fingers in autumn
When the polish of conkers and their armoured shells
Litter the ground like fallen treasure.
Silently falling leaves drift and blanket the earth.
Was that why?

I didn't know you.
I'm sorry, I don't remember your name
But I read of your story in the local paper.
You were so young
Still a child –
Yet old enough.
I saw the police cordon where they cut you down,
And the candles and flowers at the foot of the tree
Echoing the mourning of the candles above.

They cut off the branch too, as if somehow the tree were to blame.

Did you climb its strong, smooth trunk,
Hands clasped around its girth,
cheek pressed against its cool bark

and reach your way up into the canopy?
Hidden and connected –
And then connected.
Did you pause below,
Looking up into a green, enveloping dome
That cloaked you from the early morning chill and
All harm and thought beyond?

Today there are bluebells
and the warm sun dapples through the palmate leaves,
lighting up the young green of the grass.
The bark is warm and tactile, the branches strong and
 smooth,
Home and protection for many.
There is breath and space and calm and shelter.

I think that might be why.

Cwm Felin

Secret dell
Sacred fairy hollow,
Verdant green with magic.
Across the coastline, at the border between:
Sea and stone
Sky and earth
Cliff and shore
Ancient rock and ancient water,
A sheer-sided valley, a cluster of trees, the chiming of a small, clear stream -
The cloak of the Goddess over all of this.
Breath is taken at the steep descent so
You arrive as a penitent, a true pilgrim,
Gasping and in awe.
Step across the boundary of the small valley floor and all sense of the sea is lost.
No bird flight, no susurration of the waves,
No keening of the black-backed gulls beyond this shelter.
It is as if a step across this border takes you to another land.
And here instead your sight is filled with -

Green.
Mossed sycamores and ash,
Ferny shallows and grassy banks
Lichened, rusted rocks that tumble carelessly down
Across the silvered, resolute stream that laughs and
Murmurs at its approaching journey's end on the rocks of the shore beyond.

The air is translucent, fragrant,
Energised yet still and calm.
Time is suspended so you are no longer young or old
And there is nothing before or beyond this moment.
The perfumes of peaty loam and forest breath rise, eddied up
By the rush of bright water that sings along its course.
There is bird song, and the rustle of undergrowth
And if you glance from the corner of your eye
There seems to be swift movement and
Small, quick bright lights of many colours
That gloss and shimmer and are suddenly gone, not to be
    seen again,
No matter how hard you try.

The step over the stream is one of suspension,
Of the stretching of gossamer-thin boundaries between
Land and water, air and rock,
A border within this borderland,
And yet your footstep on the far bank is soft and silent.

There is temptation to linger here: other paths will always
    wait
And there is no need to rush now that time no longer matters.
It seems easier to pause in the torpid, honeyed air
And give up all thought of leaving, of growing old and
Passing from this place.
And yet.
And yet the step is taken and is followed by another,
And another, that lift you up and take you away as you begin
    your ascent on the far side of the valley.

A regretful glance over the shoulder at the closing canopy of
  green below
And suddenly you emerge on the cliff top
To wheeling gulls and the cries of kittiwakes,
The perfumes of heather and gorse mingling with the
Dusty crunch of the rocky path and the endless sea before
  you,
The touch and taste of salt-spray on your face and
The wind whipping at your hair.
The Atlantic Ocean.
Stretching away to the far horizon: green, grey, blue, black,
  white.
Constantly shifting.

All memory of the valley is momentarily wiped clean
Until a small thought is bidden forward:
That in this great expanse before you,
A tiny drop in a mighty ocean,
The soft, clear water of a silvered stream rushes freely to a
  secret cove
And gives itself up to the sea.

Bluebells

Fragile promises
cocooned in stone-aged dark,
dreaming.
Clenched nuclei biding time to burst and power,
the sacred blueprint embedded at their hearts.
Come the alchemous spring,
the vibrancy of tender green
lancing from compressed earth
is fearless in its reach.
Delicate as spindrift,
soft buds swell and colour
in the warm, forgiving sun.
Under the sheltering arms of smooth beech
and filigreed oak,
a swathe of leaf and flower
compounds to stun the senses -
colour hazing like wood-smoke as far as the eye can see,
exhalation sweet to drown the lungs
and take the breath away,
the resonance of birdsong and silence.
Sacred,
Arcane,
Fleeting,
a pure moment stilled,
that fills the heart and brings you to your knees.

Cloud Burst

Rain clouds burst into sunlight,
Scattering over the windblown city,
Turning grey-matt rooftops silver.
Telegraph wires are strung with white light
And the wind shakes new blossom
To lie sticky and forgotten,
Decaying underfoot.
Flashes of blue in the pristine sky
Spotlight fields
one by one, row after row,
As cars speed on mirrored roads,
Spray changing muddy water
To sun-flecked prisms in their wake.
And the rain makes us young again –
Fresh to start over,
Wash away mistakes and blemishes
And paint on the new,
Softening hard ground,
Rough skin,
Melting in and blending,
Lending itself to something new
And unexpected and still perfect.

And when it has seen,
When the learning and moulding
Are finished and no longer maintain
The spark of interest,
The fascination of purity,

Then it can churn and fold upon itself
And begin again.
I sit here,
Watching the raindrops
On the stained-glass dirty window,
Seeing the scudding of clouds
And the bending of the immortal trees,
And all fascinations,
All young joys,
Everything yet to be turned –
These seem muted.

Aber Mawr

Ancient and rounded as dinosaur eggs,
Pebbles as smooth as the skin on the shoulder of a child,
A kaleidoscope of size and colour,
Juxtaposed and jostling for space
And yet each set perfectly in its sole place.

These have come from mountains and sea beds,
Valley floors and glacial drifts,
Thrown up
Torn out
Tumbling down.
Born half a world away
In fire
In ice
In flood
In drought,
Tossed and gathered
Scattered and dragged
Flung and discarded.
Drawn by the gravity of an orbiting rock countless miles above
 the planet
That sets seas shifting and sighing,
Singing their way to the quiet shore.
Cast high on the bay by sullen storms,
Cruel and vicious currents leave them stranded in
Tableaux of perfect, careless elegance and harmony,
Warm and nestled in the sun.

And the susurration of the sea sets a backdrop
Of steady, constant melody against
The temporary permanence and
Humming stillness of stone.

Stump

Exposed, the leached roots look like old bone.
They have wormed and squeezed and ploughed their way
through rubble and stone, cracking concrete and wresting
apart the surety of brick
in their thirsty search for clean, clear earth,
rich loam.
Twisted, maimed and truncated,
what choice did you have?
Your trunk grew strong and fast but,
with no sure footing,
leaned,
first gently,
groomed by the sou'westerlies, nodding to their touch,
then, more heavily,
the weight of your branches dragging,
gorged and sagging with your own life's blood.

You should never have been planted here,
crushed between stone,
cornered in small suburbia.
Yours should have been a story of majesty,
of soaring rain forests, of vast hills and gorges,
strong with your brothers and sisters in serried ranks that
　claimed the landscape,
as far as the eye could see.
The songs of honeyeaters and lyrebirds,
the call of galahs and the chime of bellbirds,
these should have been yours, echoing down

across the valleys and out over the far, blued horizon
where your breath hazed the air,
breath borrowed and recycled,
seared deep into hungry lungs that suck in the clean and pure.

And now, amputated,
your remains still cling and delve,
eking and stretching,
seeking.
Each stab of the trowel
exposes more of your secrets, your story,
A forced intimacy, unwelcomed.
Yet I dig, and will do so,
until everything is bared and you have nothing left to cling to.
A tiny shoot of twig and silver-grey leaf
thrusts purposefully from your side.

I am sorry.

Lyme Bay

In the bone-warmth and solitude of this place,
Against the boundless, Impressionist canvas hung before you,
The drag and draw of the foam-laced sea lulls with its
   susurration.
In time with the beat of your heart,
The waves fold in,
Pumping and shuttering,
Aorta and valve,
Throb and drum.
Breathing slows with the evening of the pulse,
Steady and calm,
In and out,
In and out.
Salt-water waves rise and fall like the breath of the sea,
This, the only motion outside the subtle flex and poise to
   regulate against the sucking,
shifting sand between your toes,
balancing at the ebb,
The rattle and clatter of rippling pebbles
Reclaimed in the wake.

The seamless, far horizon,
The ink and turquoise sea,
Contrasts with the clear, clean focus
Of refracted light though the water where you stand.

The shine of stone, a hunted prize,
A jewel in the hand.

A black star pebble,
Compressed and polished,
That is like holding the whole night sky in your palm.
As you stand there, lulled by the sun,
It dries and fades in the warm air
Paling and waning like the course of the moon.
Sliding it back beneath the waves,
These compounded atoms,
This solid mass of carbon and gas and dust
That was spun and forged in the birth of space,
Instantly recalls its galactic heritage
And your hand lets it slip with the pull of the sea,
Leaving the magic of the universe once more beneath the waves.

Juxtaposed beside this,
You capture a flint,
The chalk edges scoured white and smudged.
Last touched by the hand of man countless thousands of years ago
As he knapped and chipped and honed a weapon,
A sharpened tool bringing death,
And with it, life.
A shard lost to the echo of the hand of a hunter,
Sea-smoothed and softened,
Blunted and decommissioned
And yet the memory of murder lies within it still,
The edge keen enough to part the skin of your fingertip,
A sliced white line that stings momentarily with sea salt.
The flint, too, slides beneath the waves,
Recalled.

And there, your magpie eye
spies a piece of sparkling sea glass,
camouflaged in the winking, aqua water,
encompassing the light of the sun.
A fragment of Roman drinking vessel, blushed with the memory of Mediterranean summer,
A shard of murderous poison bottle, deaths' secrets shattered and screaming,
A prism of costume jewellery, flawless against the pulse of a white-throated debutant,
A splinter of stained-glass window, illuminating the word of god.
Above the surface, the colours dull and bleach,
Opaque and salt stained.
The lump of once-molten sand returns to its source,
And a rainbow of light is repossessed as it flashes and shines in its sinking.

Your fingers slink into the kaleidoscopic swirl of colour again
and net a grey-silvered stone, rounded and smoothed and tactile,
Cupped in the palm of your hand like a birds' egg,
A seam of precious quartz stitched through its centre,
A geological impossibility,
this fusion of such distinct and disparate minerals.
What brought them,
colliding, compacting, fusing,
binding them for eons, never to separate until the scouring winds of the end of the earth?
They rest, these two, this one,
Conjoined,

A comforting weight; hefted lightly.
You bounce the stone softly against your palm and then
cast your prize out into the sea,
To gloop and swallow in a scatter of sun-lit spray as
the bay reclaims its own.

And over this, the weight of water,
the wait of sky.
Warm sun massages bared shoulders
and the sea and the horizon roll on forever.

Transience Blues

Wales mists brooding,
Skulking low,
Hiding ancient secrets
In the mountainous folds
Of its heather-strewn cloaks.
On lighter days than this
You can smell the purity,
Taste the colours of the gorse and bracken
And hear the swelling stream
Tinkling with such glassy, silvered insistence
That the land beneath your fingers,
Dug into your nails,
Is a malleable extension
Of your own creation.
The breath from your lungs
Shapes its silent peaks
And there is nothing more real
Than lying on your back
In the sun
In the soil
Feeling the warmth on your face
Red shadows playing behind your eyes
Darted with streaks of rapid bird flight.
To turn, roll over in the summer dust,
To feel cool moss against your cheek
And watch beetles and chew grass.

And now,
With the sky washed out,
Unpainted,
The day unfinished,
It is hard to remember how the sun feels
On outstretched fingers, teasing the soil.
Hard to envisage the lie of the
Valleys and outcrops
As the mist smokes over them,
Levelling the ground.
Heavy air silences the wash of
The swift-flowing river,
Gouging its eternal course beside me.
It holds my breath before my face
And weighs on me as if I, too,
Were mountain high.

Yet at least I have the faith
To turn from loss
And remember this,
Filling the hours with spindrift memories
Until, summoned by winking fairy fingers,
Good times come again.

Beach Light

Pellucid.
Under-lit.
The vast horizon is strata:
Dry sand
Wet rills
Surf
Sea
Sky.
Lowry figures scratch the skyline.
Your eyes shine as you race to the water
Running forever,
Speeding faster
Into your future
With me, patient in your wake,
Alone on this wide, empty beach
Whilst the thread of my heart cleaves to you
And the line draws silver-thin
Like spiders' silk.
And just as strong.

Harvest Moon, Torcross

A silk and silvered sea,
Stilled as the heat of the day leeches and diminishes
to leave a smudged-bruise horizon,
Bleeding and fading to steel,
then tin, then pewter.
Soft, the moon slides up,
Bright behind its tattering lace of cloud,
Rising and breathing as it clears the bay.
A shining copper coin,
Waxing fat and brimming with harvest and glut,
Burgeoning as it feeds on the twilight,
growing stronger and brighter as the earth turns to its calling.
A tracing fire of moonlight
sweeps across the waves,
A fey and shifting path of colour and weightlessness
that draws with the sucking of the tide and
the song of the tumbling shingle.

The stuttering, mechanical heartbeat
of the lighthouse on the Point
is a pale simulacrum,
a wan and wanting echo.

Kings Thorn

Late autumn hazes, dazes across these mountains.
They steep beside me, rendered magical with disguise
And are hued blue and violet in the subdued, yellowing sun.
Ancient trees pick out on their horizons,
Serrating the knife-point edge of the hills
And the valleys drop, slide into misted water,
Which smokes and never ripples.
Buzzards scream from the air currents above them
Swooping, stunning, scratching the air as they
Claw their way homewards, carving their way into history,
The tapestry that is the world before me.
It is told that dragons fought here - and died -
Their ancient, unfailing bodies cloaked with
Trees and evergreens,
Brambles and moss,
Shaping their way into Wales.
And should they be needed, the words must be said
And the prayers sent out to bring them home
Where they can stand, defend, protect, until
Their need is forgotten, and they melt away again.

I look behind me,
At the slumbering city.
The laced mist of these hills has changed
To polluted, soot-stained smoke,
And I look at fighting people,
The iron-ribbed road,
The jet fighters searing the sky,

The noise and traffic that spills
In a greasy overflow towards me.
I stare at this,
I speak,
I pray,
Yet the mountains do not move.
They remain aloof, immune,
And autumn mist steals in around them,
Thick as cloud,
Heavy as lead,
And shuts them away.

I turn my head.

There's a new breeze here.

Sun Down

The bruise of lilac-yellowed sky spreads,
Pink cold seeping in its wake,
And silence descends with the frost.
The town smells of Christmas
And the hands sting.
The air is still,
As if frozen as it breathes,
Smoking in the dusk.
There is no bird flight,
Nothing between me and the wide sky.
As it draws me,
The hurting broadens,
Small clouds grey and purple
As the rose-light darkens
And chilled, pale blue rises.
This is as slow or as fast
As you could want.
The fleeting permanence of evening
Grows and merges,
Swallowing as it is swallowed.
And there is nothing more than this.
Quiet, cold grey
now covers each shade
As if as new brush has taken hold,
Merging and emerging stronger,
Blanketing.

And I fall earthward.

Moonshine

The moon slides up
Like a silvered penny,
Wintered skies chill and pink beneath her,
Reaching into bones.
Skeletal trees,
Naked in the dusk,
are frozen, pasted onto alien horizons.
Even the streetlights rime,
Glazed over.
A Bethlehem blue steals in around the stars
And the city gives up,
Gives over the things it stole.
The moon shines on.

The Pool

Still
Silent
Waiting.
Mottled under pale, grey limbs,
Gloomy shadows drift on its torpid surface.
Weighted with lethargy,
Heavy as a stone,
They sink under the cloaking depths,
Dragged down,
Tugged,
Snared by monochrome fingers
That whisper promises that they will never keep.
No birds sing.
There is no breeze,
No rustling in the undergrowth.
No sunlight breaks into the tangled canopy
To cast dappled light into this woodland glade.
There is only the dark-light
Of a still pool,
A glimpse; a faint sheen,
And then it's gone.

Dare to tiptoe to the treacherous edge:

There is no reflection.

Wasteland

My name echoes to me
Across great iced wastelands
And it is lost in the wind,
No memory or force of heat
To hold it airborne.
Warmth floods from my skin,
Numbs me colder
Than the breath that freezes
Before my face,
Hollowing me.
Ice in my mind
And in my heart,
Sucked into the great white noise
That drowns.
Packed like snow,
Frozen like tears,
Driven in the wind.
The sky has no boundary,
No horizon,
And even my eyes are bleached.
A word is blown out,
Swallowed to the wilderness,
But it was never a name
I recognised.

Bird Spirit Land

A silent land bleeds white before me,
A spirit holds itself beyond my touch
And fingers draw long, lazy scars across my flesh.
There is a distant discord sound,
My voice is swallowed from my throat
Like a tongue-licked kiss to savour later.
Broken hills stumble in my eyes,
Jagged on my fingers bleed
And knowledge smokes itself into the sky.
Black-eyed crows lie bleached and silent,
Sun-stroked bones all flesh picked clean
And cradled in my hands they snap like dust.
Stone mounds restless over hollow hills,
Moan and whisper promises
That are scarcely heard and were never mine to keep.
Before my eyes blood thickens black,
The soiled hand before my face
Is as rippled as the breeze-churned lake.
I have no knowledge here to bind,
A humbled spirit floods the earth
Which lies as molten lava to my skin.
Disturbed in dreams, I live and thrive
And turn to my dismay to see destruction
From the very hands that clutch my knees.
Blackened, smoke-soiled worthless pain,
Wanton in its eager rage, consuming fire
That poisons lakes and hearts and souls within my reach.
And as I wake and see such truths

Killing me as I too kill, psychic sight betrays the fathomless grief
Where once my heart had been.

Trapeze

Swinging out into the void,
air singing.
The fine-twined strength of rope and steel,
faith in these.
Light and darkness strobe,
eyes wide,
straight ahead
the deep dark below,
too far to contemplate.
Focus
Balance
Timing.
Small adjustments,
Calculation,
but ultimately, these mean nothing.
Ahead a steady pendulum
rocking in and out of the shadows,
constant,
patient, ready,
synchronising with me -
you wait.

And I fly,
let go,
reach
fingertips outstretched.
Your sure hands are there
to clasp

and hold me skyward,
this and every other time.

No other safety net is needed.

Nectar

Like a hummingbird sipping at my breast,
Your hands, tight curled fists,
Evolve
To dimpled fat fingers that
Cradle my flesh as delicately as if it were a fine china cup.
Your free hand roams to strum my back or the pillows behind
 me
Rhythmically accompanying my heartbeat to form your
 ageless lullaby.
Your body lies, relaxed and assured, head turned,
Couched in the arms that were born to shape to your form.
I hold you to me like a brimming pot
Or as if you were the ashes of swan's bones –
Holding my breath and careful.
The blush of your cheeks
And the shadow dusting of your lashes
Are my secret happiness,
The smacks and gulps and sighs, my joy.
I scent your hair, soft and pure,
You hold my fingers, stroke my skin,
Twine my hair
As if you were my lover, not my child.
I am awed that we can do this,
Prideful that you grow and become more you
Through me.
My breasts swell and prick and spill
With the thought of you.

Joy, deeper than a well,
That you are my daughter.

Pearl

Microscopic cells,
dividing and multiplying -
and then subtracting.
A heartbeat,
Small folds of learning and processing,
Chemical equations,
complex messages,
faltering strands of DNA
twisting and linking
and then spiralling apart
with the final message to stop.
And then the slow
and hurtful parting,
Sliding away,
Tearing the fabric
to leave a small hole –
a large hole –
That couldn't be patched up.

Except,
You did leave a small part of yourself,
Clinging to the wreckage,
Embedded
and not letting go.
Not just in my secret midnight wakings
When I would almost let myself think,
feel,
But truly a part of you.

A tiny seed
to layer over and bury
shell upon shell upon shell.
And my wishful heart,
My foolish womb
Believed you and held you close,
a clutching fist,
denying all others
until time ran out
and there could be no more.

Which scrap did I cleave to?
Your still, non-beating heart?

Starman

I map out the stars.
I place my fingers on the lines
And trace cosmology.
On stilled, non-sleeping summer nights
I chart my path through
Nova and supernova,
Comets and constellations,
Planets and suns and moons.
Here, Orion's Belt; the three stars
So much like my own that they are a perfect match,
A proof of suitability.
Here, Pisces
Here, the North Star
And here, across your cheekbone,
The Great Bear.
And, silky smooth, your skin – a backdrop,
A vast galactic space on which these tracings hang.
And I, in orbit,
Gravitate to that which I call earth,
Safety,
Home.

Triptych

Light and shadow,
Plane and contour,
Three faces.
Pick out
My chin
your nose
His mouth.
The mirror melds
And separates,
Blends again.
A trick of the light
That shows your future self
And returns us to our youth.
And behind all this,
A heartbeat,
A single drum
That marks our time,
Pounding with our mingled blood,
The magic of chemistry.
A tight-drawn skin
Across a fine bone frame
That sounds
And resounds
Forever.

Guardian Angel

When I am weary, worn and sad,
Bereft of solace, stillness, love;
When I sit, slumped,
With limbs of lead,
Tension thrumming, taut hot wires,
Through veins worn lace-thin, torn and see-through.
Head down, shoulders up,
Waiting for the punch that never comes
Yet never goes away –
I close my eyes and touch defeat.

And then,
Suddenly,
You are there.

I feel your arms snake around me;
First, when you were little,
Your chubby fists would link my leg;
And then tall enough for the day
When your hands could clasp around my waist –
Cupped-fingers locked and smiling face upraised.
And now, your petal-soft skin,
Warm against my neck,
Hands crossed over my back
upon the place an angel's wings would spring from,
Against my lungs,
releasing breath,
your warm whispering in my hair.

And strength
And the hope of youth,
of life and promise
Flood me,
Radiating.
Gossamer webs of light
Linking and forging, building
An armour strong as steel.
My core
My strength
My shield.
The molten-gold centre of my heart.

You are the greatest gift I ever gave myself.

Afternoon, With Butterflies

A torpid, basking sun,
Shoulders softened under its touch,
Glinting in strands of hair as
A high breeze ghosts the treetops.

Her fingertips outstretched,
Brushing seed-heads and filaments of grasses,
Small breaths of pollen
Smoking in her wake.

The untouched meadow –
Her shadow before her, a pioneer –
Trekking virgin pathways
Into the pure unknown.

The murmuration of distant voices,
Breathing up from burgeoning gardens,
Fat with blossoms and overpowered order,
Glorious life, spilling over.

The murmur of the small stream,
Flashes of light through ethereal trees
Break and ripple, spark and bubble
On the coiling surface.

And as she walks, with every footstep that she takes,
Commas and Brimstones,
Fritillaries and Skippers,

Cloud and dance,
Rise and tremble before her
Then sigh and settle
In the deep grasses of the meadow,
Merged and masked, blended and still,

As if they were an illusion,
As if they had never been.

Forget-me-not

Forget-me-not blue, for my eyes, you said.
I know you'd searched, waiting to find just the right shade.
Warm, soft wool, twining in your fingers,
Needles clicking, knit and purl,
The alchemy of your fingertips
Changing matter,
Creating,
Re-birthing.
Measuring and holding against,
The extra-long sleeves and body that meant
I didn't have to fold myself small,
Didn't have to look out-sized,
A clown wearing little kids' clothes.
Bespoke, tailored specially for me –
No-one else could wear it –
Just mine.

Forty years ago, you knit this.
The bones of your clever fingers now dust,
The touch of your hand against my skin now cold and lost.
Long ago I spent the perfume of you
That enveloped me as I pulled it over my head.
It's saggy now.
I have to fold the sleeves.
Time has altered its structure once again.
But every now and then, I put it on
and I am warmed.
And in my reflection,

My eyes seem to blaze,
Flaring with the colour of forget-me-nots.

On Malvern

The warm breeze ripples through the gorse and teases the flesh on these hills.
She pushes back the strands of straggling hair
That the wind and heat have loosened on her face.
The ancient land stretches on, further than the eye can see:
'Seven counties on a clear day,'
'All the way to Northumberland,' –
I wonder if we can see the sea.
We listen to the mournful cries of peacocks in the valley,
Each of us haunted and baby-sad.
The wind and the dry air have rendered the surface of this immortal land to dust.
This runs before us,
Scattering, dervishing,
Changing from ancient rock to something new before our eyes.
'This is the oldest hill formation in the country,' he says,
Keeper of Knowledge of the Oldest Things.
'Imagine the glaciers that formed these valleys,
Imagine the trees that followed in their wake.'
The perfume of hawthorn blossom eddies and catches in our throats.
The earthwork hill beside us spirals in shrouded sun
And gives nothing away.
Mum counts the number of church spires, as far as the eye can see,
And tries to plot their ley lines.
The grass is worn over the much-trodden path,

And littered with rabbit droppings and lolly sticks.
The thump of bass vibrates on the wind
From the camp that the travellers have made,
Insect-like and sprawling,
At the foot of these hills.
I show the Lady of Grace the stone that I've found;
It's blue and yellow with rusted, bloody strata,
And I wonder how and why,
And she humours me and wonders with me too.
'This is a place to walk a dog,' she says,
Wistful and ghost-lost in the memory of dogs
That come at her call,
Playing at her feet,
Rolling over in the dust and bringing sticks.
This is a place to walk at night
When the hills return,
Regain the souls that they cast off for travellers,
Lest we trample them underfoot like the flowers and the ferns.
'When I die,' she says,
Sun on her face and her nut-brown arms,
'I don't want flowers,
Just buy me a seat to set on these hills.'
The pathways are strewn with old benches, metal chairs, wooden logs, new seats:
'In memory of -, who loved this place so much',
'Rest with me',
And, on the backs and arms,
'Carl luvs Julie', scratched with a penknife.
'If that's what you want, seriously now, that's what you'll have,' says Mum.

I think, it won't be much like sitting on her knee.
The ground is worn and scuffed near these benches,
Footprints clear in the dust as remembrances,
Of us, and the thousands before us.
'When I'm a ghost,' the Keeper says,
'I'll come and sit on the bench myself.'
And the ghosts of *Dorothy (known as Sally)*,
And *Beloved Mum and Dad*,
And *Mr Price*
Glide in beside us and settle the air.
'Which side of the hill?' I ask
'Oh, Hereford,' they answer.
And Worcestershire rolls out,
Patch-worked with ley-lined churches and hippy camps,
But Herefordshire rears up,
The land squashed and thrown up,
Misted and blue and more ancient.
'No wonder Elgar liked it here,' she says as we begin our descent.
An ageless, mineral sound throbs out from the British Camp
And the wind throws the distant sound of the drum-beat
And rave DJ from the travellers' convoy;
A sound that takes your heartbeat
And make you its own.
The sun filters through the trees,
Dappling the ground and snatching our shadows,
Losing us and swallowing us whole.
He talks Kipling to me,
And T. E. Lawrence,
And bears his soul as he tells me his secrets.
A tiny butterfly, bright yellow with small brown spots,

Stops and amuses for a while.
I find a feather for his hat.
And then we've circled back,
At journey's end.
'That was nice,' they say.

I wish I had taken as many pictures of them
As I did of the Hereford Hills.

Freesias

Sunlight flits across your smile
Shadow-dappling the summer of your laughter,
And we sit, side by side,
Hand in hand,
Heart to heart,
In the heat-laced garden.

The shadows of birds' dart over the climbing roses
And the perfume of freesias takes our breath away.

Time stretches forth his fading fingers
Slowly darkening the corner of this life-long garden,
But his shades will not touch us
As we sit here,
Together,
With no end and no beginning,
So eternally secure.

No word is spoken, just the hum of the bees
And the rustle of the wind softly bending the gentle heads of
  the sweet peas.
No need for quick glances as sparrow and blue-tit
Squabble in sunlight.
For we already have all we will ever need.

White Dwarf

The heart of a small star,
nucleus fading,
ashes glowing,
eating in upon itself as it burns.

The eye - a furnace,
a depth unplumbed,
a fire arrowed straight to the soul.
And the slow collapse,
the white, pulsing embers,
the small bellows catching
and faltering,
weakening,
breathless.

An undeserved diminishing.
The story of your life wiping itself clean
to leave a clear, bleached-blank page.
And then that light,
that spark,

gone out.

Memento Mori

I have a list.
Wind chimes and cake forks,
Tea trays and arum lilies,
A tract of tick boxes to telescope and summarise.
When you died,
When your bones were picked clean,
White and raw and startling,
Exposing more than the absence of flesh,
Of soul,
Prising open the frailties of your DNA
In all their vivid, bloated clarity,
I journeyed home.
The voyage now, a numbered thing,
Limited,
Precious,
Altered.
The ticking of a clock,

Winding down,

A n d t h e n

S i...

  l e n...

      t...

I needed to cling, to touch,
To harbour.
The pink elephant glass I used to clean my teeth with,
The fitting ergonomics of your watering can,
moulded to the shape of my palm,
The sewing box with the shell buttons that I played with,
The darning mushroom, it's green paint chipped with use,
The bright, coloured ribbons, coiled and tight,
ready to spring loose at a silken touch.
The Pandora perfume of the lifted lid
that drew me straight back to you,
Just yesterday -
A lifetime ago.

It was not just the losing of you,
A whole generation,
A history, gone and not returning;
Not just the fading
And the blanks,
Bleached by time,
The waning recollection of the colour of your eyes,
The lost echo of your voices,
The cooling of your fingertips.
But with it went the centre of the family,
Tearing a hollow space,
A vacuum,
A gaping void,
A sink-hole, a black hole,
With the edges collapsing in upon itself.

Your home had been our hub,

The gravitational force that
Wheeled us, orbiting,
Pulling us back for a while and then
Releasing us, flinging us,
Linked by threads of silvered light
To guide us home,
Reeling us in.
Without this centre,
This core, this nucleus,
Our atoms fly apart and scatter to the winds.
The thread no longer binds
But snaps and stutters on the breeze.
With no focus,
There is no longer the sense of needing
To gather,
To join,
To share,
To be a wider family.

It is the loss of memory
And of future.
The recollection of Scrabble at Christmas,
Of long summer evenings,
Parties on the lawns,
Christenings and birthdays
Engagements and weddings and wakes.

The house will be sold,
Shorn,
Fingered by strangers
Who won't know how that splash of paint

landed on the conservatory floor,
Who won't know the knack of jiggling the hinge
to unstick the cupboard door,
Who won't have the instinctive knowing of which of the three
  light switches in the hall is the right one.
The wallpaper you were so proud of
will be stripped.
Your bookshelves will be broken up
for firewood.
The kitchen cupboards that you made yourself,
measuring and planing, sanding and varnishing,
these will be skipped.

And so, forgive me,
If I have a list, made solid.
Memorandums,
Reliquaries
Tactile *aide memoires*,
That cup the ghost of your outlines
within their boundaries,
Encompassing,
Illustrating,
Symbolising.
Each one a story,
A silken link to
A spring morning,
A summers day,
A winter's night.
Each leather-bound book,
Each tea cup,
Each picture-frame

Is an heirloom upon which
I weave our tapestry,
our history;
Recalling you
And defining me,
Giving me form and substance.
Each trinket, a binding,
A not letting go.

You see,
It is too great,
The loss of you and the loss of the home,
Both together,
Both forever.
Irreparable,
Irreplaceable,
Gone.

I need this little list,
These small trinkets.
They are touchstones,
To help me remember the shape of myself
And the edges I must fill up to.
I need your grace,
A weeping cross,
A beacon high above a wind-swept shore,
A lighthouse,
To guide me
To the new form I must find.

Ash

The mist hangs low over
the Goyt Valley,
Like the spirits of the long-departed,
Crowding in.
Echoes of breathless voices as they
Climbed these summer hills,
The ferny, narrow gorges,
The heather-strewn hill-tops,
The music of small waterfalls,
Smoothing ancient stone and
Eddying into fathomless, peaty pools.
The scent of gorse and the soft nodding
Of fragile, sky-blue harebells and powder-pink lady's smock.
The keen panting of tongue-lolling dogs
That tangle around ethereal ankles
And then dart away to rustle in the young bracken.
The warmth of sun on freckled shoulders
And the shocking, deep refreshment
Of a sip of pure water
From a clear, babbling stream.

But today, all is still.
The heavy air cloaks all sound but birdsong,
The breeze is stilted and
The leaves of the rowan tree that waypoints our pathway
Are silent and patient.
Yet each breath taken by the living here
Is pure and deep and fresh;

Cleaning town-soiled lungs and
Filtering through the secret chambers of our hearts
And into every arcane aspect of our bodies:
Sinew; marrow; finger-tips.
I feel it.
I feel the love that you held for this place;
The joy of the free day to explore together,
The setting out on a journey,
A single step upon life's path
That would see you both still walking,
Supporting each other,
More than half a century later;
Closer then to journey's end.

And here, we carry you both now.
Pall-bearers.
The weight of the mist above us
Like the weight of the dead.
A small sack of silver-white matter:
Dust that has more substance and gravity
Than its mere physicality:
A weight that is beyond the depth of knowledge of
Newton and Einstein,
And that cannot be measured and labelled and compared.

Fragments of ash and bone,
Grey-bright and shifting
At the play of our hands underneath,
Mingling,
Mixing,
Forever joining the two component parts.

I should put a name to you.
But you are known by many names:
Son; daughter; mother; father; brother; sister;
grandfather; grandmother; wife; husband; friend.
Margaret and Alwyn.
Gran and Ga.
There.

And we: your children,
And your children's children,
And their children too;
Have brought you home,
As you wanted,
Back to these sacred hills,
Beyond the silent, cold water of the reservoir,
To a little packhorse bridge,
Spanning the soft, clear stream,
Rounded, smoothed stone underfoot
That passes and blends into
Springing grass and ancient trackway.

A grey wagtail plays downstream
And I would fancy that
There is a robin singing somewhere,
But I do not hear him now.
The air is too still and heavy for butterflies.

And we take it in turns
To tip the sack and release you,
The susurration of bone and ash
Like the releasing of a sigh;

A long-held breath;
And the soft fall of dust is
Caught by a sudden, light breeze
That streams the motes back into a column
That fancy could shape
Into shadowy outlines
And give names to -
But that is gone in an instant.

The dust rains gently into water,
Silver-white on black rock;
And swirls and clouds
Under the bridge and onwards.
Small patches of ash cling
To the stones and look like bright sun-shafts,
Piercing dark skies:
Illuminating.
Shining reflections that ripple
Through the tannin-rich water
And then are gone.

The plain, clear bag is lighter now
But there seems no end to the trail
Of ash,
Of old bone:
There is more than enough for us to scatter
In the grass by the waters' edge,
Where a natural, soft shelf would have been
Just right for you
To strip socks and stockings and
Dangle hot feet into the achingly cold

And refreshing water.
More than enough to drift through
The ferns and grass at the base of the bridge
Where you might have rested your backs
And picked a posy of
Harebells and bird's-foot-trefoil
To slip into his button-hole or
Clip into the soft curls behind her ear.

More than enough for the trickling
Against the worn stone that itself
Is crumbling in its own dust.

And it is done.

The colours stand apart and meld:
The soft, spring green of
Young ferns and fresh grass;
The black, tea-stained rocks;
The flashes of silver light
Where you rest at the end of your long travels together.

And, up by the roadside,
The rowan tree still stands sentinel,
Its heavy white flowers like blooms
Of bone-dust,
Its spreading arms
A shelter and a haven,
Protection for travellers - old and new.

The birds still sing,

The air is still pure,
The view, unspoiled.
There is peace here,
And silence.

And peace.

Published by
www.publishandprint.co.uk

Printed in Great Britain
by Amazon